D-DAY

THE FIRST 24 HOURS

D-DAY

THE FIRST 24 HOURS

WILL FOWLER

SPELLMOUNT
Staplehurst

British Library Cataloguing in Publication Data:
A catalogue record for this book is available
from the British Library

Copyright © 2003 Amber Books Ltd

ISBN 1-86227-214-X

Reprinted in 2004

First published in the UK in 2003 by
Spellmount Limited
The Old Rectory
Staplehurst
Kent TN12 0AZ

Tel: 01580 893730
Fax: 01580 893731
Email: enquiries@spellmount.com
Website: www.spellmount.com

Editorial and design by
Amber Books Ltd
Bradley's Close
74-77 White Lion Street
London N1 9PF
www.amberbooks.co.uk

Project Editor: Charles Catton
Designer: Jerry Williams
Picture Research: Lisa Wren/Natasha Jones

Printed in Italy by Eurolitho S.p.A., Rozzano (MI)

Picture credits
Amber Books: 71, 86, 99(b), 106, 131, 158(b); TRH Pictures: 2, 6-7 (US National Archives), 8, 9, 11,
13 (both), 14, 16, 18, 23, 24 (US National Archives), 25, 28 (RAF Museum), 30-31 (IWM), 32, 34
(IWM), 35, 37, 38, 39, 41, 42, 44-45 (US National Archives), 46-47, 48, 49 (IWM), 50 (US National
Archives), 51, 53, 55, 57 (US National Archives), 59 (DOD), 60, 65, 66, 68 (US National Archives),
70(IWM), 76-77 (IWM), 79, 80, 81, 82, 84 (US National Archives), 85, 87(US National Archives), 88
(US National Archives), 92-93, 94-95 (IWM), 97, 99(t), 100, 102, 104 (IWM), 107 (US Army), 120, 121,
123, 124, 128-129 (DOD), 132 (IWM), 133, 135 (IWM), 140 (USCoast Guard), 142 (IWM), 145, 158(t),
161 (IWM), 164 (IWM), 168 (IWM), 169, 174 (IWM), 175 (IWM), 177, 178-179 (US National
Archives), 181 (US Army), 185, 186 (IWM); US National Archives: 10, 26, 27, 54, 62, 75, 78, 91; John
Csaszar: 111, 114-115, 127, 138, 187; Photos12.com: (Coll-DITE-USIS), 72-73, 116, 117, 144, 183;
(KEYSTONE Pressedienst) 156-7; POPPERFOTO: 64, 119, 122, 136, 163, 165, 176, 180; Süddeutscher
Verlag: 112, 141; Topham Picturepoint: 96, 103, 166-167, 172

Map credits
Peter Harper: 20-21, 22, 43, 58, 63, 98, 110, 118, 126, 130, 134, 162, 171, 182
Patrick Mulrey: 67, 159

CONTENTS

CHAPTER ONE

THE ROAD TO OPERATION OVERLORD

The Americans pressed for an invasion of Northern Europe as early as 1942, but it would take two more years for the plans and training to reach fruition. US, British, Canadian troops and men and women from the occupied countries of Europe were now massed on a crowded island, as the Allied air forces pounded communications and defences in preparation for the invasion. Now these soldiers awaited the order to go.

BY THE SPRING OF 1944, the Western Allies and the Soviet Union knew that the war in Europe was moving, at times slowly, towards the defeat of Nazi Germany and her partners. However, they had not always enjoyed this confidence.

In September 1939, under its leader Adolf Hitler, Nazi Germany attacked Poland, and France and Britain declared war. Poland fell in a month. To secure her northern flank, Germany then invaded Denmark in April 1940 and had a tough and costly fight for Norway. In June that year, the defeat of France followed after a six-week 'blitzkrieg' ('lightning war') campaign. France was divided into a Nazi-occupied north and west and a southern 'neutral' pro-Nazi Vichy zone. In April 1941, Germany and her allies overran Yugoslavia in 11 days. Greece fell after a tough fight, and by the end of May, German

Left: Men and equipment are off-loaded from a US landing craft on a beach in Devon during a training exercise. The beaches of Devon were chosen for their similarity to the beaches of Normandy, with their long, sloping sands running gently into the sea.

paratroopers had seized the island of Crete. The Soviet Union was still bound by a 1939 non-aggression treaty it had signed with Nazi Germany, while the United States, though sympathetic to Britain, was reluctant to become embroiled in a European conflict. In the spring of 1941, Britain stood alone.

So at the beginning of Operation Barbarossa, the name of the German attack on the USSR in June 1941, and the Japanese air assault on the US fleet at Pearl Harbor in December 1941, the Axis partners of Germany, Japan and Italy enjoyed considerable military successes. In December 1941 however, the German forces were halted outside Moscow, but the following spring, four armies thrust deep into the Caucasus and reached the Volga at Stalingrad. By the winter of 1942, the German Sixth Army was embroiled in fighting at Stalingrad, while hundreds of miles to the south, at El Alamein, in the deserts of Egypt, Rommel's *Afrika Korps* had been fought to a stop by the British Eighth Army. Late 1942 was the high water mark of Nazi Germany's territorial expansion.

The British counter attack at El Alamein in October 1942 and the Soviet victory at Stalingrad in early 1943 marked the 'end of

Above: German gunners back fill sand and soil against the concrete gun pit of a 15cm (5.9in) K 18 gun in a coastal artillery position. On the right they are putting turf in place to landscape the pit, which is camouflaged from the air by a netting frame suspended over the gun.

the beginning'. Germany and her allies were now being pushed onto the defensive. North Africa was cleared of Axis forces by May 1943. British and US forces invaded Sicily in July 1943 and at about the same time, German tank forces were defeated in a massive armoured battle at Kursk in the Soviet Union.

In late 1943, the British and United Forces launched a three-pronged assault on mainland Italy and Hitler's fascist ally, Benito Mussolini, was forced out of power as Italy surrendered and re-entered the war on the side of the Allies. Fighting northwards through Italy, a country which Churchill had called 'the soft underbelly of Europe', was incredibly tough, as the Germans used natural and man-made obstacles to delay the Allied advance.

By 1944, the Allies were bogged down in front of Monte Cassino and only just holding the beachhead at Anzio. On